20TH CENTURY

Pop Culture

THE 80S

Produced by Carlton Books

20 Mortimer Street

London, W1T 3JW

Text and design copyright © Carlton Books Limited 1999/2000/2002

First published in hardback edition in 2001 by Chelsea House Publishers, a subsidiary of

Haights Cross Communications. Printed and bound in Dubai.

3 5 7 8 6 4

The Chelsea House World Wide Web address is http://www.chelseahouse.com

Library of Congress Cataloging-in-Publication Data applied for

The Early Years –1949	ISBN: 0-7910-6084-5
The 50s	ISBN: 0-7910-6085-3
The 60s	ISBN: 0-7910-6086-1
The 70s	ISBN: 0-7910-6087-X
The 80s	ISBN: 0-7910-6088-8
The 90s	ISBN: 0-7910-6089-6

20TH CENTURY

Pop Culture

THE 80s

Dan Epstein

Chelsea House Publishers

Philadelphia

20TH CENTURY

Pop Culture

The Early Years to 1949

The 50s

The 60s

The 70s

The 90s

Contents

'80

Only fifty-four percent of registered voters went to the polls for the 1980 presidential election, the worst level of turnout since Dewey nearly defeated Truman in 1948. In retrospect, such apathy was understandable; the pitiful state of the economy and Jimmy Carter's inability to resolve the Iranian hostage crisis gave voters two good reasons not to re-elect the incumbent.

In addition Ronald Reagan's blatant disregard for facts (on the campaign trail, Reagan asserted that trees caused more pollution than industry, and that new evidence had surfaced giving credence to the biblical view of creation) and the CIA connections of running-mate George Bush gave voters ample reason to be very, very frightened. In the end, Reagan's recurring cry of "**We want to be respected again**" resonated strongly with Americans shamed and frustrated by the hostage crisis; whatever happened, voters reasoned, it had to be better than another four years of Carter.

Detroit In Dire Straits

Still, if it hadn't been for Carter, Detroit would have been in even worse shape than it was by the end of 1980. On January 7, Carter signed a bill authorizing a federal bailout for the floundering Chrysler Corporation to the tune of fifteen hundred million dollars in federal loan guarantees. For Chrysler chairman Lee Iacocca, who was instrumental in swinging the deal, it was a bittersweet year; 1980 saw the introduction of Dodge's Aries and Plymouth's Reliant, the first of several successful permutations of Chrysler's "K-Car" compact, but it also witnessed the closing of Dodge's main plant in Detroit. In general, US auto sales were at their worst in nineteen years, down twenty percent from a dismal 1979; the Ford Motor Company reported a third-quarter loss of five hundred and ninety-five million dollars, the biggest ever for a US corporation.

Hollywood Highs...And Lows

Richard Pryor was also having a particularly lousy 1980. Not only did the talented comedian (who made his name with such raunchy albums as *That Nigger's Crazy* and *Bicentennial Nigger*) star in three terrible films (*Stir Crazy*, *Wholly Moses!*, and *In God We Trust*), but he also severely burned over half of his body in a **freebasing** accident. The ensuing news coverage marked the first time most Americans had even heard of freebasing cocaine.

Michael Cimino's self-indulgent *Heaven's Gate* was the talk of the industry (it cost a then-record forty-five million dollars), but for the most part Hollywood was doing very well for itself. *The Empire Strikes Back*, the second film in the *Star Wars* trilogy, was a huge hit, as was *Nine to Five*, an office comedy starring Dolly Parton and Jane Fonda. *Urban Cowboy*, starring John Travolta, started a brief western wear fad, although **Cruising** didn't exactly do the same for the

'80 Sony's Walkman, introduced in 1980, for music on the move.

'80 Lily Tomlin, Dolly Parton, and Jane Fonda plot in *Nine to Five*.

leatherman look. The film, which starred Al Pacino as a cop tracking a killer through New York City's gay bars, was the subject of vociferous protests by various homosexual organizations.

Prom Night and *Friday the 13th* were popular additions to the slasher-film genre, although **The Shining** proved that no one could swing an axe quite like Jack Nicholson. Although the

saccharine Olivia Newton-John vehicle *Xanadu* came close, none of the above were quite as frightening as *Can't Stop the Music*, a disco musical starring The Village People, Bruce Jenner, and Valerie Perrine.

Black And Blue

Neil Diamond, one of the best pop songwriters of the sixties, sank to

self-aggrandizing lows in his update of *The Jazz Singer*, although the scene with him in blackface still must be seen to be believed. Faring much better were Dan Aykroyd and John Belushi, who brought their R&B-loving **Blues Brothers** characters to the screen in John Landis' film of the same name. While Aykroyd and Belushi's own musical contributions were negligible, the film did at least give Ray Charles, James Brown and Aretha Franklin more exposure than they'd had in years.

Fashion Claims Further Victims

Reagan's election ushered in a new age of American conservatism, and the

"preppy" collegiate look popular with high school and college students fit right in with it. Sales of Brooks Brothers, LL Bean, and Ralph Lauren's Polo clothes were up, thanks partially to the publication of Lisa Birnbach's **The Preppy Handbook**. Though the book was intended as satire, it was taken at face value by most of its teenaged readers, who regarded it as a fashion bible.

Also making waves was the new, controversial ad campaign for Calvin Klein jeans. "Nothing comes between me and my Calvins," claimed fifteen year-old actress Brooke Shields (star of the risible *Blue Lagoon*), and sales of the designer jeans went through the roof.

'80 "Blues Brothers" Aykroyd and Belushi enlist Ray Charles' help in their mission.

Shotguns and Shoguns

For television viewers, "Who shot JR?" was the most important question of 1980. *Dallas* had ended its spring season with the shooting of Larry Hagman's **JR Ewing** character, and nearly everyone had a theory about who actually pulled the trigger. The November 21 episode, which provided the answer to the mystery (JR's wife's sister did it), was watched by more viewers than any other program in TV history.

Also highly rated was *Shogun*, a four-part mini-series based on James Clavell's novel of seventeenth-century Japan. The mini-series, which starred **Richard Chamberlain** as English ship captain John Blackthorne, utilized plenty of Japanese dialogue, thus introducing "Domo Arigato" to the American lexicon.

1980's popular new shows included *Flo*, a spin-off of *Alice*, *Bosom Buddies*, starring a young Tom Hanks, and *Magnum, PI*, which starred Tom Selleck as a detective living in Hawaii. ABC's **Fridays** was criticized for being a *Saturday Night Live* clone, but with the entire original cast of *SNL* gone, *Fridays* was often the funnier show of the two. *Fridays* also had a much hipper musical booking policy than *SNL*, regularly featuring bands like The Clash, The Jam, and The Pretenders.

Walter Cronkite announced his intention to retire in 1981 as anchorman of the *CBS Evening News*, a position he'd held since 1950. Mackenzie Phillips exited *One Day at a Time*, although not of her own volition; once recovered from her addiction to cocaine, she returned to the show in 1981.

Pop, Rap... And Pap

Disco continued to sell well in 1980, with songs like Blondie's "Call Me (Theme From American Gigolo)," Diana Ross' "Upside Down," Irene Cara's "Fame," and Lipps, Inc's "Funkytown" among the year's top smashes, but listeners' tastes were definitely changing. "Average Joe" rockers like Bruce Springsteen, Billy Joel, and Bob Seger were all at the height of their popularity, but mushy, adult-oriented ballads like The Captain and Tennille's "Do That To Me One More Time," Kenny Rogers' "Lady," and Christopher Cross's "Sailing" also spent time at the top of the charts. In January, The Sugarhill Gang's "Rapper's Delight" became the first rap record to make the Top Hundred, peaking at number thirty-six on the Billboard charts.

Digitally recorded LPs were widely marketed for the first time, but more important was the introduction of Sony's **Walkman** portable stereo to the United States. The lightweight tape player virtually changed the listening habits of the entire country, and was probably single-handedly responsible for the tremendous boom in cassette sales during the early half of the decade.

TOP ALBUMS

PINK FLOYD
The Wall

JOHN LENNON/YOKO ONO
Double Fantasy

THE ROLLING STONES
Emotional Rescue

BILLY JOEL
Glass Houses

BOB SEGER AND THE SILVER BULLET BAND
Against the Wind

In Arcade-ia

The videogame industry continued to thrive, with Atari still leading the pack; when the company released a home version of Space Invaders, Atari 2600 sales hit their highest level to date. Atari's first serious challenger was Mattel, who introduced a home videogame system of its own; Intellivision, which included such games as baseball, poker, and blackjack, was more expensive than Atari, but boasted better graphics. 1980 was also the year of **Pac-Man**, the most popular arcade game yet. Originally titled Puck-Man, the name was changed when Namco executives realized that vandals could easily alter the machine's lettering to read, well, something else.

Cubism

Americans who weren't glued to their videogames went nuts over Rubik's Cube, a three-dimensional puzzle invented by Hungarian architectural professor Erno Rubik *(pictured left)*. Manufactured in the states by the Ideal Toy Company, the cube sold millions; its success was quickly followed by spate of books and computer programs that could solve the puzzle for you.

Fame And Shame

In sports, the US Olympic hockey team surprised everyone by defeating the highly favored Finnish and Russian teams at the Winter Olympics in Lake Placid, New York. Muhammad Ali came out of retirement yet again, but went right back after being beaten by Larry Holmes. Rosie Ruiz, named the female winner of the Boston Marathon, was stripped of the medal eight days later when it was revealed that she took the subway for part of the race.

"This Is The End..."

Thanks to the use of "The End" in *Apocalypse Now*, a new generation of teenagers was discovering Jim Morrison and The Doors. Morrison became such a popular icon for early eighties teenagers that *Rolling Stone* was moved to do a cover story on him. The headline: **"He's Hot. He's Sexy. He's Dead."** Nobody joked much about John Lennon, however. In the weeks that followed his assassination in New York City by former mental patient Mark David Chapman, each spin of "(Just Like) Starting Over" only seemed to compound the sad irony of his death.

So Long, Colonel

December 16 was a sad day for fried-chicken lovers everywhere, as Col Harland Sanders, founder of Kentucky Fried Chicken, left for the great chicken shack in the sky. He was ninety.

'81

nineteen

When Ronald Reagan entered office in 1981, **the American economy was in sad shape.** The worldwide recession was taking its toll on an already hurting US; **inflation** rose by 14 percent, while the **unemployment rate hit 7.4 percent.** According to the Census Bureau, the average household income before taxes had declined an average of 2.6 percent per household; in a not-unrelated statistic, Americans filed for a record 1,210,000 divorces.

TOP TELEVISION SHOWS

Dallas
60 Minutes
The Dukes of Hazzard
The Jeffersons
M*A*S*H*

ACADEMY AWARDS

BEST PICTURE
Chariots of Fire
directed by Hugh Hudson

BEST ACTOR
Henry Fonda
On Golden Pond

BEST ACTRESS
Katherine Hepburn
On Golden Pond

Medical costs also hit an all-time high in 1981. *The New England Journal of Medicine* linked heart disease and coronary death to consumption of large amounts of cholesterol, and also announced that herpes simplex, the country's most rapidly spreading sexually transmitted disease, could be suppressed by acyclovir, an experimental drug. The disease that would eventually become known as **AIDS** also began to surface in 1981, killing mostly gay men in large urban areas. For the time being, it was known in medical circles as GRID, or Gay Related Immune Deficiency.

In Memoriam

In Washington DC the competition to design the Vietnam War Memorial was won by Maya Yand Lin, a twenty-one-year-old Yale architectural student. The design, a low granite V inscribed with the names of the US war dead, received mixed reviews from the public, but most Nam vets were pleased to finally receive a monument of their own. A less permanent monument was erected in Boston, when the Hostess company celebrated

the Twinkie's fiftieth anniversary by making a ten-foot-long version of the spongy snack cake. According to press reports, the über-Twinkie was filled with seventy-five gallons of creme.

Videogame News

Atari's success continued with the release of a home version of Asteroids, while newcomer Sega released an American version of Konami's popular Frogger. Video arcades in the US raked in five billion dollars in 1981, their

highest revenues to date. In other microchip news, **IBM** developed its first personal computer.

More Misery For Motown

Hard times continued to plague Detroit's auto makers; between them, they produced only 6.2 million cars in 1981, the lowest level of production in twenty years. General Motors was mired in a massive recall campaign, in which 6.4 million mid-size cars built between 1978 and 1981 had to be

returned in order to have two bolts replaced in their rear suspensions. The lone automotive bright spot of 1981 was reserved for lovers of convertibles; after several years in which no American-made convertibles were manufactured, Buick got back into the swing of things with its new Riviera Ragtop.

Fans Favour Football

The popularity of professional football was at an all-time high in 1981, as the NFL set a record attendance average of sixty thousand fans per game. Many fans were beginning to become disillusioned with baseball, especially in light of a mid-season strike by the players' union.

Victory For Video

In a landmark move, the Federal Communications Commission eased restrictions on radio stations regarding time allotted for commercials; as a result, stations could now air as many commercials as they liked, with no obligation to allocate time for news or public affairs programming. While the new ruling was a boon for radio-station coffers, it gave music fans all the more reason to turn off their radios and turn on **MTV**, the new all-music video cable channel that was, for the time being, relatively commercial free. Debuting with a transmission of the Buggles' prophetic "Video Killed The Radio Star," MTV was an immediate sensation, at least among those lucky enough to get it through their local cable service; in a move that echoed the early days of television, many bars drew in extra business by hanging "We have MTV" signs in the window. The network's original "veejays" included Alan Hunter, Martha Quinn, JJ Jackson, Mark Goodman, and Nina Blackwood. As most American recording acts (and record companies) were not in the habit of making videos, the channel was initially dominated by English artists. While this was fine for folks interested in the latest bands (and

'81 **Hall and Oates.**

fashions) coming out of the UK, many critics noticed a pronounced lack of black artists.

Black Musicians Marginalized

Caught up in the continuing disco backlash (many white record buyers now considered anything black to be "disco"), black recording artists were having a difficult time crossing over onto the pop world. "Punk-funk" king Rick James had a number three album with *Street Songs*, and a Top Twenty hit with "Super Freak," yet couldn't get his video played on MTV. **Prince**, currently racking up critical plaudits for his new *Controversy* LP, was booed off the stage at the LA Coliseum while opening for The Rolling Stones. (Within three years, a Prince show would be the most sought-after ticket in town; right now, Stones fans much preferred the bar-band blues of fellow openers George Thorogood and The Destroyers to Prince's sensual Sly Stone grooves.) Only two records by black artists topped the charts in 1981—Diana Ross

and Lionel Richie's schmaltzy "Endless Love," and "Celebration," Kool and The Gang's available-for-weddings-and-bar-mitzvahs anthem. Blondie experimented with rap in "Rapture," though rap was still too much of an underground phenomenon for the mainstream. For the most part, white America was digging the anemic arena-rock of REO Speedwagon, Styx, and Journey, the pop-country sounds of Eddie Rabbit and Dolly Parton, and the pretty-boy pop of Daryl Hall and John Oates and **Rick Springfield**. Springfield, an Australian actor and musician who'd had a fluke hit in 1972 with "Speak To The Sky," was now one of America's leading heartthrobs, thanks to his regular role as Dr Noah Drake on top-rated daytime soap opera *General Hospital*.

TV News

Two of Springfield's co-stars, Anthony Geary and Genie Francis, were the darlings of daytime TV viewers; when their characters, Luke and Laura, got married in November, the wedding

'81 *Dynasty*'s soap scandals won massive TV audiences.

REO Speedwagon

Hi Infidelity

Foreigner

4

The Rolling Stones

Tattoo You

Kim Carnes

Mistaken Identity

Styx

Paradise Theater

from Canada. The talented cast included such future film stars as John Candy, Rick Moranis, and Martin Short. Otherwise, the funniest new show on TV was *The People's Court*, a syndicated show in which real-life small claims cases were tried by retired California Superior Court judge Joseph Wapner.

Smurfs, a phenomenally popular Saturday morning cartoon concerning the adventures of blue, forest-dwelling humanoids, did appeal to certain stoned sensibilities, but the show was primarily the domain of the younger set.

Movie News

The films of 1981 were a diverse lot: Henry Fonda (in his final role) raged against the onslaught of old age in *On Golden Pond*, while Burt Lancaster played an aging gambler in Louis Malle's bleak *Atlantic City*. Superman (Christopher Reeve) married Lois Lane (Margot Kidder) in *Superman 2*, while an inebriated Dudley Moore charmed Liza Minelli in *Arthur*. Already popular for his *Star Wars* appearances, Harrison Ford became a major star on the strength of **Raiders of the Lost Ark**, Steven Spielberg's exciting throwback to the days of Saturday afternoon serials.

Kathleen Turner made a stunning debut in Lawrence Kasdan's *noir*-ish *Body Heat*, while Faye Dunaway's

episode scored the highest ever rating largest for a daytime dramatic series. In the wake of *Dallas*, **nighttime soaps** were poping up everywhere; *Dynasty*, starring Linda Evans and John Forsythe, and *Falcon Crest*, starring Robert Foxworth and Ronald Reagan's former spouse Jane Wyman, were two of the most popular.

Bored with the stale skits of *Saturday Night Live* and *Fridays*, many viewers began to switch their late-night allegiances to **SCTV Network**, an innovative and surreal comedy show

Olivia Newton-John

"Physical"

Kim Carnes

"Bette Davis Eyes"

Diana Ross and Lionel Richie

"Endless Love"

Daryl Hall and John Oates

"Kiss On My List"

Christopher Cross

"Arthur's Theme (Best That You Can Do)"

portrayal of Joan Crawford in *Mommie Dearest* was so over the top ("No more wire hangers, *ever!*") that audiences didn't know whether to laugh or recoil. Burt Reynolds sleepwalked through another series of uninspired films (*The Cannonball Run*, *Paternity*, *Sharky's Machine*), but he could seemingly do no wrong in the eyes of the moviegoing public. Warren Beatty, on the other hand, fell flat with *Reds*, an overlong romance set against the Russian Revolution. The **horror genre** continued to thrive, with films like *Friday the 13th Part Two*, *Halloween Two*, *Happy Birthday to Me*, *My Bloody Valentine*, *An American Werewolf in London*, and *Scanners* all doing well at the box office despite their variable quality. The year's biggest horror, however, was Brooke Shields' listless performance in Franco Zeffirelli's *Endless Love*; it was slowly dawning on the public that, though beautiful, Brooke couldn't act her way out of a bag.

John Waters would have known what to do with Brooke Shields. Notorious for such cult gross-outs as *Pink Flamingos* and *Desperate Living*, Waters had a knack for putting familiar faces in unexpected roles. *Polyester*, Waters' first mainstream film, featured such oddball casting choices as 1950s teen idol Tab Hunter and Dead Boys vocalist Stiv Bators, as well as a scratch-and-sniff "Odorama" gimmick. It also, like most of Waters' best films, starred 300-pound transvestite **Divine**, this time in the role of a suburban housewife.

'81 Harrison Ford in cracking form as Indiana Jones in *Raiders of the Lost Ark,* and Faye Dunaway (*above*) in *Mommie Dearest*.

'82

Whether it was due to "Reaganomics," or just the result of the economy running its natural course, inflation dropped to six percent in 1982. Unemployment, however, continued to climb, hitting 10.8 percent by the end of the year. A record 4.6 million people were on unemployment by October. Over thirty banks failed, and interest rates went through the roof.

Meryl Streep and Kevin Kline star in *Sophie's Choice*.

Despite the drop in inflation, Detroit was still hit hard by the popularity of imports, which now comprised thirty-five to forty percent of the entire US auto market. Ford tried to improve matters by releasing its 1983 Mustang, which sported a rounded "aero" look that bore little resemblance to its predecessors; though not a failure, the change in styling didn't exactly kickstart sales. Independent auto maker **John De Lorean** got the worst news of all in the fall, when he was busted by federal agents for participation in a twenty-four-million-dollar cocaine deal.

Things were much sunnier over at **EPCOT Center**, the latest addition the Disney World theme park in Orlando, Florida. A geodesic dome featuring educational exhibits with futuristic themes, EPCOT (ie, Experimental Prototype Community of Tomorrow) immediately boosted attendance at the park.

PR Falls In Videogame War

Apple Computer had reason to celebrate in 1982, becoming the first personal-computer firm to reach one billion dollars in annual sales. Atari, on the other hand, was running into trouble. First the company released a home version of Pac-Man, but its cheap graphics and poor playability rendered it extremely unpopular. Then Atari introduced its new 5200 system, an updated version of the Atari 2600; unfortunately, as the 5200 was initially incompatible with 2600 game cartridges, customers had to buy all new games. The company eventually got around to releasing a 2600/5200 adapter, but it came too late to repair the public relations damage.

Other companies were only too happy to capitalize on Atari's mistakes. Coleco released ColecoVision, a programmable home system with the best graphics and sounds to date,

ET the amiable alien captured Americans' hearts.

while General Consumer Electronics (GCE) released **Vectrex**, the first home console system to incorporate vector graphics technology. Midway introduced Ms. Pac-Man, which proved even more popular down at the arcade than its predecessor; despite this, arcade revenues were down from the previous year, a trend that would continue during the next fifteen years.

Out Of This World

Hollywood had one of its best years yet, with profits up nine percent from 1981. Much of these profits, of course, came from the success of **ET** *The Extra-Terrestrial*, Steven Spielberg's heartwarming tale of a lost alien boy. Other big money-makers included **Tootsie**, a comedy starring Dustin Hoffman as an actor who pretends to be a woman in order to get work, and the melodramatic *An Officer and a Gentleman*, starring Richard Gere and Debra Winger. Tobe Hooper, leaving the low-budget gore of *The Texas Chainsaw Massacre* behind him, made *Poltergeist*, a ghost story as scary as it was successful at the box office.

Arnold Schwarzenegger returned "to hear ze lamentations of ze women" in **Conan the Barbarian**, the popularity of which inspired a whole string of broadswords-and-biceps epics. Sylvester Stallone also had ample opportunity to flex his pecs, thanks to **Rocky III** (in which he fought the mohawked-and-muttonchopped Mr T and jogged through endless training montages to the

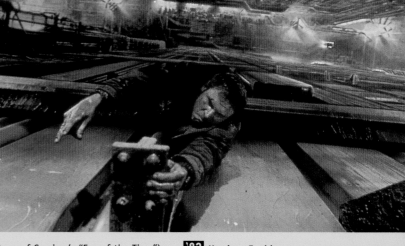

'82 Harrison Ford hangs on in *Blade Runner*.

tune of Survivor's "Eye of the Tiger") and *First Blood*, the story of a Nam vet squaring off against smalltown police.

Burt Reynolds was still America's most popular leading man, even if his film choices (*The Best Little Whorehouse in Texas*, which also starred the massively popular Dolly Parton, and *Best Friends*) were dubious at best. In *Fast Times At Ridgemont High*, Sean Penn attracted plenty of attention as a stoned troublemaker named Spicoli, while little-known actors Mickey Rourke, Kevin Bacon, Ellen Barkin, and Paul Reiser all gave impressive performances in Barry Levinson's **Diner**. Meryl Streep gave a typically breathtaking performance as a holocaust survivor in *Sophie's Choice*.

Tron, starring Jeff Bridges as a computer expert trapped in a giant videogame, was notable only for its computer-generated special effects. **Blade Runner**, Ridley Scott's disturbing vision of the not-so-distant future, failed at the box office despite the presence of Harrison Ford, though it has since become a cult favorite. Even more disturbing was the X-rated

'82 "Thief. Warrior. Gladiator. King." A sword-wielding Arnie plays Conan the Barbarian.

IN THE NEWS

January 26 – In his State of the Union address, President Reagan proposes turning over such federally funded social programs as welfare and food stamps to the individual states. Reagan cites this as an example of "New Federalism."

February 6 – Reagan's proposed budget for the upcoming fiscal year asks for huge cuts in domestic spending, but asks for an 18 percent increase in military spending.

March 10 – The US imposes economic sanctions on Libya, in response to the country's involvement with terrorist organizations like the Palestine Liberation Organization.

June 21 – John Hinckley, Jr found not guilty by reasons of insanity for shooting President Reagan and three others. Hinckley, who was obsessed with actress Jodie Foster, believed that he could impress her by killing the president.

June 25 – Alexander Haig resigns as Secretary of State following disagreements with Reagan and his cabinet.

BEST PICTURE

Gandhi

directed by Sir Richard Attenborough

BEST ACTOR

Ben Kingsley

Gandhi

BEST ACTRESS

Meryl Streep

Sophie's Choice

Café Flesh, in which "positives" perform sex acts for the enjoyment of "negatives," who cannot participate. Though often seen as a prescient analogy for the AIDS epidemic to come, the film could easily have been inspired by the wave of genital herpes then sweeping the country—By the end of 1982, twenty million Americans were thought to have the sexually transmitted disease.

Tragedy hit Hollywood twice in 1982. On March 5, hard-partying **John Belushi** died in a bungalow at the Beverly Hills Hotel; an autopsy ruled that his death was caused by a lethal dose of heroin and cocaine. On July 23, Vic Morrow and two child actors were killed in a helicopter accident on the set of *The Twilight Zone*. Director John Landis and four others were indicted on charges of involuntary manslaughter, but later acquitted.

A Blast From The Ghetto

Little noticed in 1982 was an independent film called *Wild Style*. Directed by Charlie Ahearn, the film explored the burgeoning rap music, breakdancing and graffiti art scenes in the black community of New York's South Bronx. Grandmaster Flash and the Furious Five, one of the rap acts to appear in the movie, released a 1982 single called "**The Message**." A departure from the group's usual party-down chants, "The Message" was the first rap hit to comment on the social issues and pressures facing urban blacks; though not a huge pop hit, the single crossed over just enough to let white folks know that something interesting was afoot in the ghettos of America.

For the most part, 1982 was a pretty dull year for American music. Hall and Oates and Lionel Richie continued to dominate the charts; heartland rocker John Cougar found success with watered-down Springsteenisms; and seventies faves like Steve Miller and Chicago came back for another helping of consumer dollars. There were a few highlights, however. Joan Jett (former guitarist for The Runaways, the controversial all-girl band managed by LA entrepreneur extraordinaire Kim Fowley) kicked some real rock 'n' roll back into the charts; The Blasters and The Stray Cats reintroduced American kids to the joys of rockabilly; and The Go-Go's, products of a wide-ranging LA punk scene that included The Blasters, The Circle Jerks, and Black Flag, had melodic guitar-pop to spare. **Frank Zappa** teamed up with his daughter Moon Unit for "Valley Girl," a novelty song which parodied the "val-speaking" residents of LA's San Fernando Valley, and actually gave Zappa the biggest hit of his career.

Liberace's Frame Claim

After a couple of decades' absence, Liberace was back in the headlines when Scott Thorson, his chauffeur and "companion," filed a lawsuit against the flamboyant entertainer. Although Thorson, who had recently broken up with Liberace, really only wanted his belongings back, the press had a field day trumpeting the case as a "palimony" suit. Liberace, for his part, denied being gay, telling journalists that he was the victim of a homosexual conspiracy.

TV News

Introduced in February, *Late Night with David Letterman* was an immediate hit; though Letterman and Johnny Carson were contracted to the same network, many felt that the irreverence of *Late Night* was a much-needed antidote to the increasingly predictable *Tonight Show*. Thanks to recurring appearances by Larry "Bud"

JOAN JETT AND THE BLACKHEARTS

"I Love Rock N Roll"

PAUL MCCARTNEY WITH STEVIE WONDER

"Ebony and Ivory"

SURVIVOR

"Eye Of The Tiger"

J GEILS BAND

"Centerfold"

DARYL HALL AND JOHN OATES

"Maneater"

Melman and Chris Elliot and regular features like "Stupid Pet Tricks," *Late Night* became *the* show to discuss around the office water cooler.

Cheers was another long-running favorite that debuted in 1982; the

'82 Joan Jett.

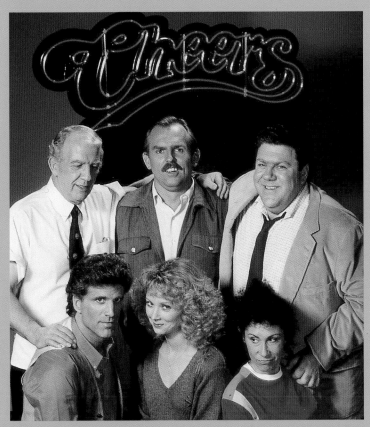

'82 The cast of *Cheers*.

sitcom, which followed the lives of a handful of regulars at a Boston bar, starred Ted Danson and Shelley Long. Less enduring was *Joanie Loves Chachi*, a dull *Happy Days* spin-off starring Scott Baio and Erin Moran.

Knight Rider, starring former soap star David Hasselhoff, certainly took the prize for the most unlikely premise: An undercover cop (played by Hasselhoff) is killed, brought back to life by a reclusive millionaire, and given a new identity and a Pontiac Trans Am with a talking computer. Believable? Hell, no. Popular? Hell, yes.

Now that the hysteria over Luke and Laura's wedding had died down, *General Hospital* star Tony Geary capitalized on his newfound name-recognition by appearing in ads for the **"Members Only"** line of men's jackets. Unfortunately, as Geary's TV character was somewhat disreputable,

his endorsement only confirmed what many already believed—that "Members Only" jackets were for sleazebags.

Big On Broadway

Big-budget Broadway productions proliferated in 1982, thanks in part to the success of Andrew Lloyd Webber's

lavish *Cats*, which opened October 7 at the Winter Garden in New York City. Harvey Fierstein's *Torch Song Trilogy* finally made it to Broadway after a successful off-Broadway run, and *Little Shop of Horrors*, a musical based on the 1960 Roger Corman film of the same name, opened at the New York's WPA Theater to rave reviews.

NFL Strikes Out...

A year after the divisive players' strike, major league baseball was back in top form, setting an attendance record of 44,500,000. This year, it was the NFL's turn to go on strike; the walk-out lasted from September 21 to November 16, cutting the season to nine games apiece per team.

...And Fonda Feels The Burn

Aerobic excercise was becoming increasingly popular, with *Jane Fonda's Workout Book* topping the best-seller list, and as a result, headbands and workout clothes became a regular sight outside of gyms as well as in.

'82 *Knight Ride*r David Hasselhoff.

TOP ALBUMS

MEN AT WORK
Business As Usual

ASIA
Asia

JOHN COUGAR
American Fool

THE GO-GO'S
Beauty and the Beat

FLEETWOOD MAC
Mirage

83

Tensions were rising in Lebanon, relations with the Soviet Union were growing ever more strained, and the invasion of Grenada gave Ronald Reagan's approval ratings a quick shot in the arm. But for most Americans, 1983 would forever be remembered as the Year of the Cabbage Patch Doll (*below*). No two of the pudgy, stuffed-cloth dolls looked exactly alike; their handmade construction meant that supplies were limited, and kept prices prohibitively high.

TOP TELEVISION SHOWS

60 Minutes

Dallas

Dynasty

Magnum, PI

Simon and Simon

Still, every child had to have one—or so the media claimed. In actuality, it was the parents who were going crazy over the doll; in the possessions-conscious atmosphere of the early eighties, it became a virtual badge of honor to be wealthy enough to shell out the required $125, and tenacious enough to hack your way through the mini-riots occurring inside toy stores which had the dolls in stock.

Conspicious Consumption

But the Cabbage Patch Doll was just the proverbial tip of the iceberg; not since the Eisenhower years had America reveled in such unapologetic materialism. The rise of the "**Yuppie**" class was partially to blame, as young urban professionals ostentatiously stocked their condominium apartments with expensive appliances and the latest in high-end stereo and video gear, and drove to work in shiny new Benzes and Beamers. Additionally, the Reagan administration's barely concealed contempt for the poor gave tacit approval to those who viewed abundance as their inalienable right. The have-nots weren't going away, however; America's poverty rate was at its highest level in eighteen years, with over thirty-five million citizens living below the poverty line.

Watt A...!

1983 was also the year that US Secretary of the Interior James Watt talked himself out of a job. Already despised by conservationists for his scorched-earth attitude towards the environment (like Reagan, he also seemed to believe that trees were the primary cause of the country's pollution problem), Watt became embroiled in further controversy for speaking out against a planned Beach Boys' Independence Day concert at Washington DC's Washington Monument; Watt feared that the band would attract "the wrong element" to the nation's birthday celebration. Watt put his foot in his mouth for the last time in October, when he was forced to resign over publicly describing a newly appointed coal-lease commission as consisting of "a black, a woman, two Jews, and a cripple." National Security Adviser William P Clark was named as his replacement.

Beauty Queen Loses Her Crown

Controversy also swirled around Vanessa Williams (*above*), a stunning twenty-year-old from New York. Not only was Ms Williams the first black woman to win the Miss America pageant, but she was probably also the first Miss America to have posed nude for lesbian- and bondage-themed photos. Yielding to extreme pressure from pageant officials, Vanessa abdicated her throne after the pictures (which had been taken the previous year) appeared in an issue of *Penthouse*.

Detroit Battles On...

The Chrysler Corporation regained its financial footing in 1983, thanks to the introduction of Dodge's 1984 Caravan and Plymouth"s 1984 Voyager, America's first mini-vans. The vehicles, which could seat up to eight people, became the eighties equivalent of the family station wagon. Lincoln, usually the very definition of excess, did an about-face with the 1984 Continental Mark VII, a semi-fastback coupe with smoother, more rounded styling than any Continental before it. Priced between twenty-two and twenty-five thousand dollars, the Mark VII aimed squarely (and successfully) at the Yuppie demographic, which was currently paying twice as much for high-priced imports like BMW.

...But Atari Ships Out

Atari had a difficult year in 1983; oversaturation of the home videogame market was hurting everyone's sales, but buyers increasingly seemed to favor Mattel's Intellivision or Coleco's ColecoVision. Looking to cut costs, Atari was forced to move its operations overseas, and the company never quite regained its hold on the market.

'83 Vanna White says little but reveals all.

TV News

With cocaine abuse on the rise in the US, First Lady Nancy Reagan took a hands-on approach to the problem by making an appearance on a "very special" episode of *Diff'rent Strokes* (any time a sitcom episode dealt with serious issues such as drugs, sexual abuse, or the evils of punk rock, it was invariably advertised as "very special"). The solution, the First Lady told Little Arnold (Gary Coleman), was simple: **"Just say no."** Upon hearing these sage words of advice, a nation of freebasers would presumably throw down their bunsen burners, never to get high again.

Really, who needed drugs when you had **Star Search**? A talent contest for aspiring singers, dancers, actors, comics and "model/spokespersons," hosted by by Johnny Carson sidekick Ed McMahon, *Star Search* was so banal as to be positively hallucinatory. A year after its debut, the show actually made a star out of singer Sam Harris, who briefly pierced the Top Forty with the disturbingly titled "Sugar Don't Bite."

Another "very special" television event was the November 20 broadcast of **The Day After**; the made-for-TV movie, about the effects of nuclear conflagration, was watched by an estimated 100 million viewers. An even larger audience—125 million—tuned in for the final two-and-a-half-hour episode of *M*A*S*H*; after eleven years on television (most of them spent at the top of the ratings), the men and women of the 4077 said farewell to the Korean War. *After MASH*, which debuted

IN THE NEWS

April 11 – A presidential panel recommends the installation of 100 ICBM missiles in silos in Wyoming and Nebraska, as well as the development of the single-warhead "Midgetman" missiles.

April 18 – The US embassy in Beirut, Lebanon is almost completely destroyed by a car bomb. Pro-Iranian terrorists are blamed in the blast, which kills 63.

May 24 – Congress approves spending $625 million on the research and development of MX missiles.

June – Homosexuals across the country march in protest of what they view as the media's sensationalization of AIDS, which to date has killed over 600 Americans.

September 5 – The US imposes light sanctions against the USSR (including suspension of negotations for a US embassy in Kiev) over the Soviet downing of a South Korean passenger airliner.

in the fall, followed the post-war adventures of several *M*A*S*H* characters, but the show failed to hold the interest of even the most diehard *M*A*S*H* fans.

Beauty And The Beast

Wheel of Fortune, the highest-rated daytime game show in TV history, went into syndication in 1983. The latest incarnation of the show was hosted by Pat Sajak, but letter-turner **Vanna White** became the program's most popular attraction, despite the fact that she rarely (if ever) said

angled for an Oscar by directing herself in *Yentl,* but the film (about a young Jewish woman who disguises herself as a man in order to study the Talmud) proved more popular with Jewish senior citizens groups than with Academy members.

A Star Is Reborn

Shirley MacLaine had better luck, nailing an Academy Award for her role as the mother of dying daughter Debra Winger in *Terms of Endearment.* MacLaine also published *Out on a Limb* in 1983; the book, an account of her involvement with various forms of spirituality, would have been met with ridicule a decade earlier, but now many Americans were acquainting themselves with "New Age" concepts.

Scarface, a cocaine-laden update of the 1932 gangster classic, was criticized for being too violent, while *Staying Alive,* the Sylvester Stallone-directed sequel to *Saturday Night Fever,* was widely assailed for being just plain terrible. Worst of all, according to those who actually

anything. Vanna later posed for *Playboy,* and her fascinating auto-biography, *Vanna Speaks!,* became a best-seller.

Mr T cashed in on his memorable appearance in *Rocky III* with a role on the popular new adventure show, *The A Team.* Born Laurence Tureaud, the gold-bedecked Mr T soon had an entire country imitating his gruff cry of "I pity the fool!" But the year's most unlikely new TV idol had to a dog by the name of **Spuds MacKenzie**; billed as "The original party animal," Spuds did little in his commercials for Bud Light beer except let scantily clad

models fawn over him (or her; a small scandal erupted when it was revealed that Spuds was actually a bitch). Nevertheless, Spuds merchandise (T-shirts, posters, statuettes) quickly became big business, and Spuds was regularly mobbed during personal appearances at bars and taverns.

Movie News

Though 4.1 million VCRs were sold in 1983, and subscribers to cable TV now numbered over twenty-five million, Hollywood barely felt the pinch, thanks to the popularity of *The Return of the Jedi, Terms of Endearment,* and *The Big*

Chill. Tom Cruise danced around in his underwear in *Risky Business,* Meryl Streep played a reluctant nuclear activist in *Silkwood,* and Jennifer Beal's **Flashdance** wardrobe inspired a vogue for torn-collared, off-the-shoulder sweatshirts; combined with a headband and brightly colored leg-warmers, the look was quintessentially eighties.

Jerry Lewis, who had made only one film since his 1972 pet project, "The Day the Clown Cried" (about a clown who cheers up children at Nazi prison camps) failed to find release, made a rare return to the silver screen in *The King of Comedy*. Barbra Streisand

ACADEMY AWARDS

BEST PICTURE
....
Terms of Endearment
....
directed by James L Brooks
....

BEST ACTOR
....
Robert Duvall
....
Tender Mercies
....

BEST ACTRESS
....
Shirley MacLaine
....
Terms of Endearment

MICHAEL JACKSON
Thriller

THE POLICE
Synchronicity

LIONEL RICHIE
Can't Slow Down

Flashdance
soundtrack

QUIET RIOT
Metal Health

caught it during its brief stay in the theaters, was *The Lonely Lady*, a trashy vehicle for would-be actress **Pia Zadora**. The multi-talented Pia did at least score a minor hit in 1984 with "And When The Rain Begins To Fall," a duet with Jermaine Jackson.

Music News

Jermaine's brother Michael was the

THE POLICE
"Every Breath You Take"

MICHAEL JACKSON
"Billie Jean"

IRENE CARA
"Flashdance ... What A Feeling"

PAUL MCCARTNEY AND MICHAEL JACKSON
"Say Say Say"

LIONEL RICHIE
"All Night Long (All Night"

'83 Al Pacino plays a trigger-happy gangster in *Scarface*.

music business's most valuable player in 1983. *Off The Wall*, his 1979 LP, had been a huge success, but it seemed like small potatoes next to *Thriller*. The album boasted no less than six Top Ten hits ("Billie Jean," "Beat It," "Wanna Be Startin' Somethin," "Human Nature," "PYT," and the title track), and Michael's face (with its suspiciously altered-looking nose) seemed to be on MTV twenty-four hours a day. *Thriller* eventually went on to sell forty million copies, breaking nearly every industry record in the process.

Colleges Rock

Metal Health, an album by LA rockers Quiet Riot, presaged the coming popularity of heavy metal (spandex-trousers-and-big-hair version), while Styx's overblown *Kilroy Was Here* signified the last gasp of prog-rock concept albums. Talking Heads, a New York-based art-rock combo, cracked the Top Ten with "Burning Down The House," while **REM** (right), an enigmatic quartet from Athens, Georgia, made it into the Top Forty with *Murmur*, despite receiving very

little commercial air-play. College stations, on the other hand, were playing the hell out of *Murmur*; record companies reasoned that there might be more gold in them thar hills, and thus REM's success single-handedly paved the way for the rise of "college rock." It also led to the rediscovery of **The Velvet Underground**, a band REM regularly cited as an important influence. By 1985, all of the Velvet Underground's records were back in print, and were selling far better than they had back in the late sixties; no

September 20 – Congress authorizes US marines to remain in Lebanon for another eighteen months.

October 23 – A truck loaded with explosives destroys the US Marine headquarters in Beirut, killing 241 Marine and Navy personnel.

October 25 – In response to a bloody coup by pro-Marxist guerillas, US forces invade the Caribbean island of Grenada. Hostilities end on November 2, with eighteen US soldiers dead and 115 wounded.

November 2 – President Reagan signs a bill designating a federal holiday to honor the late Dr Martin Luther King, Jr.

November 11 – The US sends the first of 160 cruise missles to Great Britain; in response, the USSR withdraws from arms limitation negotiations.

December 3 – Syrian forces near Beirut fire on US reconnaissance planes, prompting an attack from US warplanes the following day.

longer would they be remembered only as "that band Lou Reed was in before *Walk On The Wild Side*."

'84 "Like A Virgin"—Madonna, and (right) Run DMC.

'84

Having won re-election by the largest Republican landslide in history, President Reagan interpreted his massive victory as a "mandate" to run the country in whatever manner he deemed necessary. In actuality, Reagan was re-elected on the strength of the economy, which was at its healthiest since 1951.

TOP TELEVISION SHOWS

Dynasty

Dallas

60 Minutes

The A Team

Simon and Simon

Certainly, most Americans would have been hard pressed to rationalize the inherent contradictions in the Reagan administration's foreign policy: At the same time the US was sending military aid to El Salvador, in order to help the established Salvadorian government fend off insurgent forces, it was also supporting the Contra rebels trying to topple Nicaragua's Marxist Sandanista government. (Reagan even showed his solidarity with the Contra "freedom fighters" by posing for photo ops while wearing an "**I'm A Contra, Too!**" baseball cap.)

Rising Population Triggers Boom

In any case, people were buying new homes again; 1.7 million homes were built in 1984, the most since 1979. Of course, the prison construction business was booming as well; over 454,000 Americans were doing time, nearly double the total from a decade ago. The US population swelled to 236,158,000 in 1984, with most of the growth taking place in the South and West. Chicago, traditionally known as

'84 Popular cop Eddie Murphy.

"The Second City," had its role as the country's second largest city usurped by Los Angeles. People were also buying cars. Detroit's "Big Three" auto makers earned nearly ten billion dollars in 1984, an industry record. Riding high on his company's bust-to-boom turnaround, Chrysler chairman **Lee Iacocca**'s *Iacocca: An Autobiography* began a two-year run at the top of the best-seller list.

Big And Beefy

The 1980s ushered in a new age of hostile corporate takeovers, and they didn't come much bigger than Beatrice Foods' purchase of Esmark, Inc. for $2.8 billion. The deal made the Chicago-based Beatrice the second largest food and consumer product company in the world, and the company proudly trumpeted the fact with its appropriately Orwellian "**We're Beatrice**" ad campaign, which covered everything from orange juice to tampons. Wendy's Hamburgers launched its enormously successful "**Where's the Beef?**" TV ads, which provided America with a new buzz-phrase (men's underwear emblazoned with "Here's the Beef!" became big sellers at lingerie shops), and gave elderly character actress Clara Peller her fifteen minutes of fame.

Bell Go Over Big

Good news for the eight percent of American households that owned personal computers: Bell Laboratories announced the development of a megabit memory chip, capable of storing more than one million bits of electronic data. Bad news for the videogame industry: No longer able to bear the glut of games, home systems and other related products, the videogame market crashed hard. Atari 2600 software could be found in the budget bins of supermarkets everywhere; fearing a similar fate, Mattel and Coleco hurriedly got out of the videogame business. Many observers opined that the videogame fad had reached the **"game over"** stage.

Running On Air

Sales of home exercise equipment passed the billion-dollar mark, as the fitness industry continued to boom. Then again, being in good shape wasn't everything, as Jim Fixx found out; at the age of fifty-two, the fitness guru (and author of the best-selling *Running*) dropped dead of a heart attack—while running, of course. 1984 also saw the introduction of Nike's Air Jordans, basketball shoes endorsed by the Chicago Bulls' phenomenal Michael Jordan.

Movie News

Breakdancers were everywhere in 1984—from TV commercials and music videos to the opening ceremonies of LA's Summer Olympics, if it didn't feature someone spinning on their head, it just wasn't happening. Hollywood moved quickly to cash in on the fad, releasing four low-budget **"breaksploitation"** flicks (*Beat Street, Body Rock, Breakin'* and *Breakin' 2: Electric Boogaloo*) before the year was out. Barely three years old, MTV was already exerting a powerful influence on the music and film industries. The quick edits and garish lighting that were an integral part of music videos now found their way into films as varied as *Beverly Hills Cop* (starring Eddie Murphy), *Footloose* (starring Kevin Bacon), Walter Hill's *Streets of Fire*, and *Purple Rain*, Prince's screen debut. Record and movie executives also realized that, by integrating scenes from a current film into a music video, you could sell a movie *and* its accompanying soundtrack, effectively killing two birds with one stone. Still, the combination of music and film didn't necessarily guarantee a hit. *Rhinestone*, in which Dolly Parton tried to turn Sylvester Stallone into a country singer, was too stupid for even the most undemanding viewers, while **This Is Spinal Tap**, Rob Reiner's "mockumentary" of a

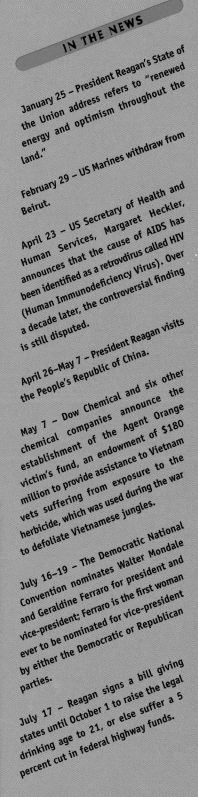

IN THE NEWS

January 25 – President Reagan's State of the Union address refers to "renewed energy and optimism throughout the land."

February 29 – US Marines withdraw from Beirut.

April 23 – US Secretary of Health and Human Services, Margaret Heckler, announces that the cause of AIDS has been identified as a retrovirus called HIV (Human Immunodeficiency Virus). Over a decade later, the controversial finding is still disputed.

April 26–May 7 – President Reagan visits the People's Republic of China.

May 7 – Dow Chemical and six other chemical companies announce the establishment of the Agent Orange victim's fund, an endowment of $180 million to provide assistance to Vietnam vets suffering from exposure to the herbicide, which was used during the war to defoliate Vietnamese jungles.

July 16–19 – The Democratic National Convention nominates Walter Mondale and Geraldine Ferraro for president and vice-president; Ferraro is the first woman ever to be nominated for vice-president by either the Democratic or Republican parties.

July 17 – Reagan signs a bill giving states until October 1 to raise the legal drinking age to 21, or else suffer a 5 percent cut in federal highway funds.

'84 Spoof rock-doc *Spinal Tap*— almost too convincing.

continued to sell by the truckload; in addition, he also found himself roped into singing the hook on Rockwell's "Somebody's Watching Me," and appearing (and doing the bulk of the work) on The Jacksons' *Victory* tour. Michael *had* to work hard, though; unlike the previous year, he had some serious competition this time around. In *Purple Rain,* Prince had both a blockbuster film and a multi-platinum album, while Bruce Springsteen's **Born In The USA** took him almost overnight from basketball arenas to eighty-thousand-seat football stadiums. Tina Turner's comeback was so strong that her Ike and Tina years seemed like a

faded British metal band, may have been too subtle for its own good; members of several preview audiences were heard to ask, "How come they didn't make a movie about a *good* band?" The film became a cult hit among musicians, however, and rare indeed is the guitarist who can't recite Nigel Tufnel's **"This one goes to eleven"** routine in its entirety.

In fact, most of 1984's biggest films had little to do with music. *Indiana Jones and the Temple of Doom* earned forty-two million dollars in the first six days of its release, despite a weak script and a shrill performance by Kate Capshaw as Harrison Ford's love interest. Pat

Morita taught Ralph Macchio to stand up for himself in *The Karate Kid,* while Melanie Griffith played a porno star caught up in a murder mystery in Brian De Palma's *Body Double.* The one-two punch of *The Terminator* and *Conan The Destroyer* turned **Arnold Schwarzenegger** into a superstar, and John Hughes' *Sixteen Candles* marked Molly Ringwald as an actress to watch.

What A Nightmare!

Slasher films were so formulaic by 1984 that any semblance of creativity was usually reserved for their ad campaigns: *Silent Night, Deadly Night*

featured an axe-wielding Santa and the slogan "He knows when you've been naughty," while print ads for *Pieces* opted for a picture of a chainsaw and the subtle tag-line, "You *know* what it's about!" Into this gory and redundant fray came Wes Craven's *A Nightmare on Elm Street;* while certainly flawed, audiences responded to the film's hallucinatory images and Robert Englund's frightening turn as the blade-fingered Freddy Krueger.

Music News

Like Big Brother himself, Michael Jackson was everywhere in 1984. Stoked by Jackson's million-dollar video for its title track, *Thriller*

TOP ALBUMS

PRINCE AND THE REVOLUTION
PURPLE RAIN
soundtrack
FOOTLOOSE
soundtrack

BRUCE SPRINGSTEEN
Born In The USA

HUEY LEWIS AND THE NEWS
Sports

MADONNA
Like A Virgin

July 18 – James Huberty shoots and kills 21 people at a McDonald's in San Ysidro, Caliornia, before being shot and killed by police officers. Huberty's widow, Etna, files suit against McDonald's, claiming that her husband's rampage had been caused by an overdose of Chicken McNuggets.

August 20–23 – The Republican National Convention renominates Reagan and Bush.

September 20 – A car bomb kills 23 people at the US Embassy in Beirut.

October 7 – Walter Mondale wins his first presidential debate with Reagan, who seems disoriented and unclear on certain facts. A better-prepared Reagan performs more effectively at the second debate, on October 21.

October 11 – Dr Kathryn D Sullivan becomes the first woman astronaut to walk in space.

November 6 – Ronald Reagan is re-elected president by nearly 17 million votes.

December 22 – Bernhard Goetz, a self-employed engineer, shoots four black teenagers on a New York subway. Goetz, who had been brutally mugged in 1981, claims that they demanded money from him; many consider the so-called "subway vigilante" to be a hero. Goetz eventually receives a one-year prison sentence—for illegal gun possession.

mere warm-up, while newcomers Madonna and Cyndi Lauper quickly became the idols of millions of girls for their independent attitudes and bag-lady fashion sense.

Head Bangers

Heavy metal was back with a vengeance. Eddie Van Halen's blazing guitar solo on "Beat It" had helped Michael Jackson cross over to rock radio, but it also turned a lot of pop fans on to Van Halen, the band; *1984*, the band's final album with extroverted frontman David Lee Roth,

was its most successful yet, spawning the popular singles (and videos) "Jump," "Panama," and "Hot For Teacher." Fellow Sunset Strip denizens Ratt and Motley Crue got heads banging with *Out Of The Cellar* and *Shout At The Devil*, respectively, while Twisted Sister's years of toiling in Long Island bars paid off with the Top Twenty-Five single, "We're Not Gonna Take It." Rocking hardest of all was "Rock Box," an inspired stew of street raps and metallic guitars from New York rap duo Joseph Simmons and Darryl McDaniels, better known as RUN-DMC.

Soul Giant Gunned Down

Plagued for years by drug and tax problems, Marvin Gaye made a major comeback in 1983 with "Sexual Healing." Gaye was working on the follow-up to his successful *Midnight Love* LP when, on April 1, he was shot and killed by his father during an argument. It was a sad and ignominious end to one of soul music's greatest singers.

The Right Prescription

Comedian Bill Cosby already had plenty of hit movies, TV series, and records under his belt by 1984, but nothing on his resume even came close to matching the runaway success of **The Cosby Show** (above). A family-oriented sitcom based around the everyday lives of the Huxtables, an upper-middle-class black doctor's family in Brooklyn, New York, *The Cosby Show* became the most popular series, comedy or otherwise, of the 1980s. Also debuting in 1984 was long-running mystery series *Murder, She Wrote*, starring Angela Lansbury, and *Who's the Boss?*, a popular sitcom featuring former *Taxi* star Tony Danza. The new **Miami Vice** came off like a slick cross between a cleaned-up *Scarface* and a music video, and became an immediate hit; *Dreams*, starring John Stamos, tried to incorporate the MTV vibe into a sitcom format, and barely lasted a month. With *Little House On The Prairie* and *Bonanza* behind him, Michael Landon scored his third popular series in a row with **Highway to Heaven**. The story of an angel who comes down to

earth to help people, *Highway To Heaven* was singled out by President Reagan as one of the year's best shows.

1985 was the year that Mattel's Barbie, kitted out with business suit and briefcase, joined the ranks of the young urban professionals; her new outfit reflected the fact that, for the first time in history, the majority of professional positions were now held by women. The good news for Barbie and her colleagues was that the **US economy continued to grow**, albeit at a slower rate than in 1984, and that the **unemployment rate of 6.8 percent** was the country's lowest in nearly five years.

TOP TELEVISION SHOWS

The Cosby Show
Family Ties
Dallas
Dynasty
60 Minutes

ACADEMY AWARDS

Out of Africa
directed by Sydney Pollack

BEST ACTOR
William Hurt
Kiss of the Spider Woman

BEST ACTRESS
Geraldine Page
The Trip to Bountiful

'85 *Left:* **Cher, dressed to kill at the Academy Awards, and (***below***) Stallone shoots to kill in** *Rambo.*

But for the first time since World War One, America owed more to other countries than it was owed; in reponse, the US, Great Britain, France, West Germany, and Japan took steps to devalue the dollar 4.29 percent against other currencies. In addition, thanks primarily to the Reagan administration's cuts in funding for mental institutions, America's homeless population was climbing dangerously close to the one million mark.

Gung-Ho Heroes Gross Highest Profits

Movie profits were down seven percent in 1985, a drop which was widely blamed on the increasing sales of VCRs and the rise of video rental stores. Still, it was hardly like people were avoiding the theaters. *Back to the Future* (a sci-fi comedy starring *Family Ties'* Michael J Fox), *Witness* (with Harrison Ford as a policeman hiding out in Pennsylvania's Amish community), *The Color Purple* (Steven Spielberg's controversial adaptation of Alice Walker's novel about the life of a Southern black woman), and *Out of Africa* (in which Robert Redford and Meryl Streep found romance against the backdrop of early-twentieth-century Kenya) were all enormously successful at the box office, as was the Schwarzenegger shoot-'em-up *Commando*. Sylvester Stallone climbed into the ring yet again in *Rocky IV*, but it was **Rambo: First Blood Part II** that made the biggest impression on American viewers. Released during the tenth anniversary of the Vietnam War, *Rambo* (about a Nam vet who returns to Cambodia to rescue American MIAs) exploited the country's continuing inability to come to terms with losing the conflict; failing to beat the Viet Cong on the battlefield, America could now at least exact revenge (over and over again) on the silver screen. The film was an immediate smash, and Ronald Reagan publicly praised Rambo as "America's Hero." A similar "back to Nam" premise turned the **Chuck Norris** action vehicles *Missing in Action* and *Missing In Action 2—The Beginning* into box-office bonanzas, and Norris also found time to whup him some Commie ass in *Invasion USA*, which (like 1984's *Red Dawn*) was an un-ironic throwback to the Cold War paranoia of the 1950s. *Gymkata* was even more gloriously absurd, starring diminutive Olympic gymnast Kurt Thomas as a US agent

using a singular style of martial arts ("The skill of gymnastics—The kill of karate!") to complete a mission in an Albania-like kingdom.

A popular regular guest on *Late Night With David Letterman*, Pee-wee Herman (aka Paul Reubens) scored a screen hit with *Pee-wee's Big Adventure*, while Madonna played a character resembling her current public image in *Desperately Seeking Susan*. Cher was not nominated for an Academy Award for her part in *Mask* (in which she played the mother of a severely deformed teenaged boy), but she easily won "Most bizarre getup" on Oscar Night with her Bob Mackie-designed outfit (one hesitated to call it a dress) and matching frightwig.

John Hughes, who had tallied previous hits with *Mr Mom*, *National Lampoon's Vacation*, and 1984's

Sixteen Candles, was now one of Hollywood's most successful directors: *National Lampoon's European Vacation*, *Weird Science*, and *The Breakfast Club* were all hits in 1985. The latter film, starring Emilio Estevez, Judd Nelson, Molly Ringwald, Anthony Michael Hall, and Ally Sheedy, marked the rise of "**The Brat Pack**," an aggregation of up-and-coming young actors, many of whom also appeared (along with Rob Lowe,

'85 Brat Packers play teens from Shermer High in *The Breakfast Club*.

Demi Moore, and Andrew McCarthy) in 1985's *St Elmo's Fire*. Although much hyped at the time, none of the Brat Packers (with the possible exception of Demi Moore) would go on to have anything approaching a distinguished career.

RIP Rock

On October 2, Rock Hudson became the first high-profile figure to die of AIDS. His futile search for a cure focused some much-needed attention on the growing epidemic; his former lover, Marc Christian, later successfully sued Hudson's estate, claiming that Hudson had jeopardized Christian's life by refusing to admit to his condition during their relationship.

Cool CD's

In music, 1985 was the year of Live Aid, Farm Aid (a Live Aid-style concert benefitting America's economically embattled farmers), and the founding of the Rock and Roll Hall of Fame, established in the rock 'n' roll hotbed of Cleveland, Ohio. It was also the year of the **compact disc**; despite being substantially higher-priced than turntables and LPs, CD players and CDs were immediately so successful that many predicted vinyl would be rendered completely obsolete by the end of the decade. Sales of vinyl singles were also down substantially, due to the introduction of the "cassingle" format.

Musicians Take Moral Stance

Rock music came under fire in 1985 when the **PMRC**, a self-appointed moral watchdog committee formed by the wives of several prominent politicos, began to pressure record companies to save the youth of America by putting warning stickers on records containing "**offensive**" lyrical content. Despite the popular image of rockers as anti-establishment rebels, Frank Zappa and Twisted Sister's Dee Snider were the only prominent musicians with the courage to appear at the PMRC hearings; both men spoke eloquently of their opposition to the album-labeling plan. Unsurprisingly, the music industry knuckled under with a minimum of fuss, and twenty-two record companies pledged to slap parental warnings on any product containing potentially offensive material. Ironically, the careers of previously obscure bands The Mentors and WASP experienced a sudden boost, after the song lyrics to their respective "Golden Showers" and "Animal (F*ck Like A Beast)" were read aloud at the PMRC hearings.

Don't Give Up The Day Job

Former Credence Clearwater Revival leader John Fogerty returned after an absence of over a decade with the best-selling *Centerfield* LP, acclaimed underground bands The Replacements and Hüsker Dü signed deals with major labels, and a brash youngster named **LL Cool J** established himself as rap's newest superstar with the block-rockin' debut album *Radio*. But for the most part, the airwaves seemed to be filled with faceless pop (Starship's "We Built This City," Mr Mister's "Broken Wings"), syrupy ballads (Whitney Houston's "Saving All My Love For You," Lionel Richie's "Say You, Say Me"), and songs with tie-ins to current films (Madonna's "Crazy For You," John Parr's "St Elmo's Fire," Huey Lewis and The News' "The Power of Love"). **Eddie Murphy**, one of the funniest men in America, made a misguided attempt at a career in music; although the sung-

'85 David Bowie, Alison Moyet, Pete Townsend, Bob Geldof, and Paul McCartney—stars supporting the starving in Live Aid.

with-the-utmost-seriousness "Party All The Time" made it to number two in the charts, the Rick James-produced single proved that, as a vocalist, Eddie was one hell of a comedian.

Razor-Sharp Style?

If Madonna was single-handedly popularizing the crop-top-and-exposed-bra look for young women, Don Johnson's *Miami Vice* wardrobe was similarly influential on the male clothing styles of the day. With *Miami Vice* high in the ratings, it suddenly became the height of fashion to wear pastel-colored, European-cut sports jackets with solid T-shirts and baggy, beltless pants. Special razors that could help you attain Johnson's "permanent stubble" look were also briefly marketed, but never really caught on—even though Bruce Willis, of TV's new *Moonlighting*, also sported a pretty serious five o'clock shadow. A screwball comedy loosely based on the 1940 film *His Girl Friday*,

Moonlighting quickly became a viewer favorite for its knowing wit and the obvious chemistry between Willis and co-star Cybill Shepherd.

Other popular new shows in 1985 included *MacGyver*, an adventure series starring Richard Dean Anderson as a resourceful secret agent; *The Golden Girls*, which starred Bea Arthur, Betty White and Rue McClanahan and was the first successful TV sitcom with an all-female cast; *Growing Pains*, a sitcom starring Alan Thicke (whose late-night talk show, *Thicke of The Night*, had been one of 1983's most critically savaged programs) as a psychiatrist working out of his Long Island home; and *Puttin' on the Hits*, a mind-numbing game show that featured contestants lip-synching to their favorite pop songs.

US Says Yes To NES...

Pronounced dead the year before, home videogames started to make a comeback, thanks to the new Nintendo Entertainment System. Burned by the recent videogame crash, retailers were initially reluctant to stock the NES, but the popularity of Nintendo titles like Donkey Kong, Super Mario Brothers, and The Legend of Zelda soon revitalized the industry.

...But No To New Coke

The biggest marketing gaffe of the decade occurred on April 23, when the Coca-Cola Company, in an attempt to fend off the rapidly expanding Pepsi-Cola, suddenly replaced its venerable Coca-Cola soft drink with the heavily hyped New Coke. From Coke loyalists, the howls of outrage were immediate and deafening; the new, sweeter formula tasted too much like Pepsi, they said. Despite the outpouring of criticism, the company stubbornly stood by its new product, even as

'85
"Cop Chic"—*Miami Vice*.

newspapers ran story after story of people making car trips to other cities and states where old Coke was still available, in order to stock up before supplies ran out forever. Finally, the utter failure of the new product forced the company to relent, and the old formula was brought back on July 10, under the name of **Coca-Cola Classic**. Coca-Cola continued to try to push New Coke, but to no avail; like the Ford Edsel before it, New Coke was an improvement that no one had asked for, and it was quietly withdrawn from the shelves before the decade was out.

'**nineteen**

'86

With only two years remaining in his presidential career, Ronald Reagan decided that the **Strategic Defense Initiative** would be a nice little something for Americans to remember him by. Nicknamed "Star Wars" for maximum soundbite value, the missile defense system could supposedly destroy enemy missiles before they struck American targets, thanks to a complex network of missiles, ground-based lasers, and particle beam sensors that would be **stationed in outer space.**

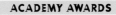

ACADEMY AWARDS

BEST PICTURE

Platoon

directed by Oliver Stone

BEST ACTOR

Paul Newman

The Color of Money

BEST ACTRESS

Marlee Matlin

Children of a Lesser God

TOP TELEVISION SHOWS

The Cosby Show

Family Ties

Murder, She Wrote

Cheers

60 Minutes

'86 Angela Lansbury, star of *Murder, She Wrote.*

In July, Senate budget cuts considerably slowed the SDI's development, but Reagan would not let go; in October, a summit meeting between the US and the Soviet Union ended in a stalemate, solely because Reagan refused to even consider limiting or delaying the "Star Wars" program any further.

Contra-Dictory

Unfortunately for the president, there were more pressing issues to worry about. The "**Iran-Contra scandal**," as it came to be known, began in November with rumors that the US had sold arms to Iran, with the understanding that Iran might be able to influence Lebanon to release its

'86 "Top Gun" Tom Cruise takes Kelly McGillis' breath away.

American hostages. Though Reagan had claimed to be virulently against trading arms for hostages, American intelligence sources confirmed that the sales had indeed taken place. Reagan first admitted that he knew of the arms sale, then quickly backpedalled, saying he didn't really understand the full extent of the situation.

Things got even more complicated on November 25, when it was revealed that some of the profits from the Iranian arms sale had been diverted to the Nicaraguan Contras. National Security Council adviser John Poindexter hurriedly resigned, while his assistant, Lieutenant Colonel Oliver North, was fired. On November 26, Reagan appointed a "blue ribbon" panel, headed by former senator John Tower, to investigate the actions of North and the National Security Council.

Movie News

While Oliver North was being investigated, Oliver Stone was being feted. *Salvador* and *Platoon*, both of which were written and directed by Stone, were two of the year's most critically praised films; the latter picture, based on Stone's own experiences as a soldier in Vietnam, was also the director's first major commercial success. The low-budget comedy *She's Gotta Have It* was another critical and commercial hit, with **Spike Lee** winning praise as one of America's most promising young directors. John Hughes continued his string of teen-oriented successes with *Pretty in Pink* and *Ferris Bueller's Day Off*.

'86 Spike Lee—a director to watch.

Tom Cruise was America's hottest star in 1986, playing a pool hustler in *The Color of Money* and a hot-shot jet pilot in **Top Gun**. Bette Midler was filmdom's most popular female, thanks to leads in the hit comedies *Down and Out in Beverly Hills* and *Ruthless People*, while Sigourney Weaver took on an army of slimy extra-terrestrials in *Aliens*. Arnold Schwarzenegger played yet another wise-cracking, ass-kicking tough guy in *Raw Deal*, but the failure of *Cobra* seemed to indicate that audiences were only interested in seeing Sylvester Stallone as Rocky or Rambo. The "Comeback of the Year" award went to **Dennis Hopper** (*below*, with Isabella Rossellini) who played three troubled (but extremely diverse) characters in *Hoosiers*, *River's Edge*, and David Lynch's *Blue Velvet*—the latter of which featured him as the oxygen-swilling Frank Booth, one of the most genuinely frightening psychopaths in film history.

Not Just For Kids

Based on one of Stephen "Just call me the Master of Horror" King's short stories, **Stand by Me** was actually a moving study of childhood friendship; directed by Rob Reiner, the film brought a talented young actor named River Phoenix into the public eye. *Crossroads*, starring Ralph Macchio, could easily have been titled *The Karate Kid Plays the Blues*; with Ry Cooder overdubbing his parts, Macchio challenged the Devil (guitar whiz Steve Vai) to a battle of the blues that surely had Robert Johnson spinning in his grave. In other child actor news, over one hundred X-rated videos starring porn star **Traci Lords** had to be pulled from the shelves, when it was revealed that Lords made them while still under the age of sixteen.

Out Of Their Heads

By June of 1986, 21,915 cases of AIDS had been reported in America, over half of them already fatal. Officials predicted that the number of

IN THE NEWS

January 7 – President Reagan announces economic sanctions against Libya, in response to that country's alleged involvement in terrorist attacks on the Rome and Vienna airports.

January 28 – The space shuttle Challenger explodes 74 seconds after liftoff at Cape Canaveral, Florida. All seven of the crew members are killed, including schoolteacher Christa McAuliffe, the first private citizen to participate in a space shuttle flight. The failure of a seal on a solid-fuel rocket booster is blamed for the accident, which ignites public debate on whether or not America should continue to develop its space program.

March 24 – Libya launches a missile attack on US Navy vessels in the Gulf of Sidra; the US fleet responds with missile attacks that damage a Libyan missile site and destroy two Libyan patrol boats.

March 25 – Congress approves $20 million in military aid to Honduras, where Nicaraguan Contra rebels have set up bases just inside the country's border.

April 5 – 60 Americans die as a bomb explodes in a West Berlin discotheque. US officials blame Libya for the bombing.

April 14 – US launches an air strike against Libya in retaliation for the April 5 bombing in West Berlin.

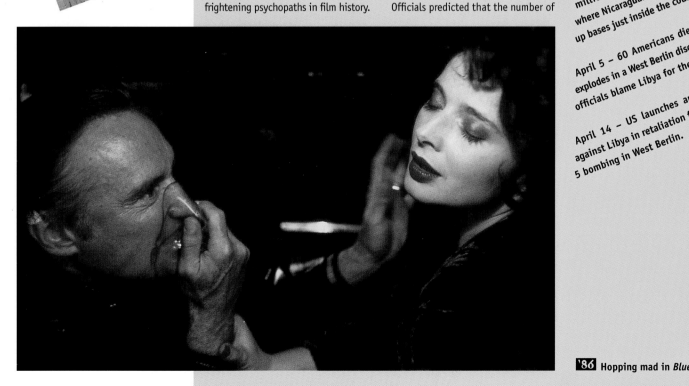

'86 Hopping mad in *Blue Velvet*.

deaths from AIDS would increase more than tenfold over the next five years. Predictably, the network news shows were more interested in the country's escalating drug problems, especially in light of the cocaine-related deaths of college basketball star Len Bias and professional football player Don Rogers. During one week in September, CBS and NBC each tried to out-coke the other, CBS leading with the news special "48 Hours on Crack Street," while NBC followed up with the news special "Cocaine Country."

ALF was one of the year's most popular new sitcoms. Short for "Alien Life Form," ALF (played alternately by a puppet and by midget Michu Meszaros) was a furry alien who crash-landed on Earth (below), and decided to shack up with a suburban family; hilarity and "wry" commentary on human ways ensued. *Pee Wee's Playhouse*, a highly creative Saturday morning series starring Pee Wee Herman, took the opposite approach, transporting kids (and quite a large

number of adult fans) into a surreal world of talking furniture, friendly robots, and disembodied heads. If that wasn't weird enough for you, there were always those California Raisins commercials, in which a soul train of finger-poppin' raisins sang "I Heard It Through The Grapevine."

Videogame News

In the world of videogames, Nintendo still ruled the roost. Sega introduced its new Sega Master System in 1986, while Atari tried to relive past glories with its new 7800 console, but Nintendo's NES still outsold both products by a margin of ten to one.

Music News

With her third album, *True Blue*, Madonna shortened her tresses and generally tried to "class up" her image, a move no doubt motivated by her recent marriage to actor Sean Penn, with whom she made the virtually unwatchable *Shanghai Surprise*. **The Bangles**, an all-female quartet with roots in LA's early-eighties "paisley underground" scene (which included such neo-psychedelic combos as The Three o' Clock, The Dream Syndicate, and Rain Parade), had two massive pop hits in 1986 with "Manic Monday" (written by Prince) and "Walk Like An Egyptian." **Bon Jovi**, who sounded like a cross between Bruce Springsteen and a metal band, scored a pair of chart-toppers with "You Give Love A Bad Name" and "Livin' On A Prayer." **Metallica**'s thrash-metal classic *Master of Puppets* made it into the Top Thirty without the benefit of any commercial radio support, but their momentum was lost when bassist Cliff

Burton died in a bus crash during the band's Swedish tour.

Miami Vice's Don Johnson scored a Top Five hit with "Heartbeat," although he seemed much more comfortable in front of a camera than a microphone. Janet Jackson, younger sister of Michael, stepped out on her own with *Control*, while James Brown entered his fourth decade of hits with the success of "Living In America." Paul Simon's use of South African musicians on his new *Graceland* LP inspired a flurry of interest in "world music," while **Run DMC** further fused rock and rap by teaming up with Aerosmith for a revamp of the latter's "Walk This Way." All was not well in the rap world, however; regular reports of violence (gang-related and otherwise) at rap shows caused many big-time concert promoters to steer clear of rap acts.

Missing Links

If 1985 was the summer of Live Aid, 1986 was supposed to be the summer of Hands Across America. The event, which was supposed to raise money for the homeless, involved forming a human chain that would stretch across

the country from New York City to Long Beach, California. Unfortunately, the whole thing was completely disorganized; on the day of the event, endless stretches of ribbon had to be substituted for human beings in many parts of the country.

86 Girl band The Bangles.

The Young Pretender

On November 22, Mike Tyson, aged just twenty, became the youngest heavyweight boxing champion in history, knocking out Trevor Berbick in the second round of the WBC heavyweight title fight.

Power Trips

Sixteen million cars and trucks were bought by Americans in 1986; only 28.2 percent of them were imported, a smaller percentage than in previous years. Chevrolet gave Corvette buffs a reason to celebrate with the release of the first Corvette convertible in a decade; just in case buyers needed any further incentive, Chevrolet raised the car's horsepower to two hundred and forty, up ten from their previous models. General Motors, the largest American company with business interests in South Africa, made headlines in October by withdrawing its operations in protest of the country's apartheid policies. Following GM's lead, IBM, Eastman Kodak, and Citibank would all do the same over the course of the next twelve months.

'86 "Iron" Mike Tyson becomes heavyweight champion.

May 13 – A Justice Department commission on pornography, headed by Attorney General Edwin Meese, rules that such material is potentially harmful and can lead to violent behavior against women and children. The Meese Commission urges stringent action against the pornography industry, and puts pressure on convenience stores to remove magazines like *Playboy*, *Penthouse*, and *Hustler* from their shelves.

June 17 – Chief Justice Warren Burger retires from the US Supreme Court. Reagan names the more conservative William Rehnquist as his successor, and also names Antonin Scalia to the court.

July 27 – The International Court of Justice orders the US to stop training and arming Nicaragua's Contra rebels, and to pay restitution to Nicaragua.

October 22 – Reagan signs a revised federal income tax law, lowering taxes for everyone, especially those in the highest tax brackets, as of January 1, 1987.

November 3 – A Lebanese magazine reports that the US has been secretly selling arms to Iran, in hopes of securing the release of US hostages currently being held in Lebanon.

November 14 – Financier Ivan Boesky agrees to pay the government $100 million as a penalty for illegal insider trading on the security exchange. The Securities and Exchange Commission bars Boesky from participating in the securities business for the rest of his life, although he is allowed to liquidate stocks in order to pay off the $1.4 billion debt still owed by his firm. Boesky is also sentenced to three years in prison.

nineteen

'87

However sordid it may have seemed at the time, 1987 was certainly one of the most entertaining years in recent memory.

If Gary Hart's extramarital indiscretions, the Iran-Contra hearings and Reagan's endless wranglings over Supreme Court nominees couldn't get you to crack a smile, there was always the endless saga of televangelist Jim Bakker to keep you amused.

A long with his wife, the mascara-caked Tammy Faye, Rev Bakker ran the Soutch Carolina-based PTL ministry, one of the most prominent of the country's many televised pulpits. On March 19, Bakker shocked his flock by resigning, having admitted to an extramarital affair with church secretary Jessica Hahn. Bakker's troubles were only beginning; on June 12, the PTL's new management filed for bankruptcy, and later sued Bakker for helping himself to over fifty-two million dollars from the ministry's coffers. Finally, in October of 1989, Bakker was convicted on twenty-four counts of fraud and conspiracy, and sentenced to forty-five years in prison (the sentence was later reduced to a far more lenient four and a half years). Along with the 1988 sex scandal involving televangelist (and Bakker rival) Jimmy Swaggart, the PTL affair went a long way towards diminishing the power of the religious right in America.

'87 Michael Douglas succumbs to fatally attractive Glenn Close.

North Comes Clean

If Iran-Contra was supposed to be the Watergate of the eighties, someone forgot to tell the congressional committee investigating the affair. The televised congressional hearings, which ran from May 5 to August 6, were marked by the Democrats' unenthusiastic cross-examination of witnesses, while the Republican panelists mostly used the hearings as a forum for pro-Contra rhetoric. Though obviously set up as a **fall guy** by the Reagan administration, Lt Col Oliver North nonetheless

defended the the administration's involvement in the affair. Fawn Hall, North's attractive secretary, received numerous offers to pose nude for men's magazines.

Black Monday

The worst stock crash in the history of the New York Stock Exchange occured on October 19, when the Dow Jones industrial average fell 508 points in heavy trading. The panic quickly extended to markets around the globe, but the blame could be laid squarely at the doorstep of the US's enormous trade deficit.

Just as Three Mile Island kick-started the box-office success of *The China Syndrome* in 1979, the "Black Monday" crash was the best advance publicity that Oliver Stone's *Wall Street* could have asked for. Stone's gripping morality tale starred Michael Douglas as sleazy trader Gordon Gekko, whose motto, "**Greed is good**," perfectly encapsulated the dominant philosophy of the era. Douglas also starred in the popular *Fatal Attraction*, as a married man whose weekend fling (Glenn Close) turns out to be a raving homicidal looney. Eddie Murphy returned as Axel Foley in *Beverly Hills Cop II*, and also made an uncredited cameo appearance in *Hollywood Shuffle*, Robert Townsend's comedic look at racial stereotyping in the film world. Arnold Schwarzenegger continued his string of successes with *The Running Man* and *Predator*, while *Over the Top*, Sylvester Stallone's idiotic arm-wrestling epic, only extended Sly's post-*Rambo* slump. Cher had her best year yet, garnering raves for three roles—as a public defender in *Suspect*, as one of a trio of

gorgeous witches in *The Witches of Eastwick*, and as a young widow torn between two brothers in *Moonstruck*. Barbra Streisand bombed with *Nuts*, but Faye Dunaway made an impressive comeback as a gin-mill moll in *Barfly*, Barbet Schroeder's film based on the writings of Charles Bukowski; Mickey Rourke wasn't bad in the Bukowski role, either. Having played small roles for his entire career, Kevin Costner began to take himself extremely seriously after his turn as Eliot Ness in *The Untouchables* made him a star. Robert De Niro, who played Al Capone in *The Untouchables*, also played the satanic Louis Cyphre in *Angel Heart*, a film which got plenty of publicity mileage out of a nude scene by *The Cosby Show*'s Lisa Bonet. **Patrick Swayze**, best known for films like *Skatetown, USA*, and *Red Dawn*, became a full-blown heartthrob after playing a hunky dance instructor in *Dirty Dancing*.

Music News

With sales of over 102 million in 1987, the CD market continued to swell. Industry bean-counters had been counting on *Bad*, Michael Jackson's highly anticipated follow-up to *Thriller*, to make a serious contribution to year-end sales figures, and they weren't disappointed. While *Bad* wasn't quite the all-encompassing smash that its predecessor was, it still sold eight million copies and generated five Number One singles, including "Man In The Mirror" and the title track.

"Who's better—Tiffany or Debbie Gibson?" was the question upon the lips of young record buyers everywhere (not to mention several pop culture

IN THE NEWS

March 4 – In a televised address, Reagan takes "full responsibility" for the Iran-Contra affair, but stops short of admitting that the plan was wrong.

March 20 – The federal government approves the use of AZT (azido-thymidine) on AIDS patients. Tests show that AZT may help AIDS patients live longer, although the drug is criticized by some for its expense ($10,000 per year per patient) and its many side effects.

May – Democratic presidential hopeful Gary Hart drops out of the race after allegations surface about his womanizing.

May 17 – An Iraqi warplane mistakenly fires two missles at the USS Stark in the Persian Gulf, killing 37 US sailors. Iraq apologizes for the incident.

July 22 – US warships begin escorting Kuwaiti oil tankers through the Persian Gulf to protect them from Iranian attacks.

August 18 – The Food and Drug Administration approves the trial use of a possible AIDS vaccine.

October 1 – Los Angeles is rattled by an earthquake measuring 6.1 on the Richter Scale. Eight people die, and over 100 are injured.

December 8 – Reagan and Gorbachev sign the first US-Soviet treaty to reduce nuclear arsenals. According to the agreement, 2,611 US and Soviet medium- and short-range missiles are marked for destruction.

December 22 – Barred by International Court of Justice from sending any further arms or military supplies to the Nicaraguan Contras, Reagan authorizes $14 million in "non-lethal" Contra aid.

observers with nothing better to do). Sixteen-year-old shopping mall diva Tiffany topped the charts with a cover of Tommy James' "I Think We're Alone Now," and the seventeen-year-old Gibson placed her own compositions "Only In My Dreams" and "Shake Your Love" in the Top Five.

Some older folks got in on the pop action, as well: The venerable **Grateful Dead** scored their first Top Ten hit with "Touch of Grey". Bruce Willis took advantage of his *Moonlighting* fame by croaking his way through *The Return of Bruno*, a collection of R&B chestnuts. His cover of "Respect Yourself" made it to number five on the charts—seven positions higher than the Staple Singers' original hit in 1971. Slayer's Kerry King shredded some additional guitar on *Licensed To Ill*, the debut LP by New York's white rap trio **The Beastie Boys**. Stoked by the runaway success of "(You Gotta) Fight For Your Right (To Party!)," *Licensed To*

Ill sold 5 million copies, becoming the first rap record to top the pop album charts.

In August twenty thousand fans from around the world rolled into Memphis to observe the tenth anniversary of Elvis Presley's death. 1987 witnessed the passing of Liberace and Andy Warhol, the former from AIDS and the latter from complications following a gall bladder operation. Both these men had an incredible influence on popular music—Liberace with his outrageous sense of onstage style, and Warhol with his concepts of self-reinvention.

Family Dramas

The brand new Fox network made a run at becoming the Big Three's hold on network television, thanks to the success of **Married...with Children**. Many found the show's characters repugnant in the extreme, but others felt it was a breath of fresh air in a world of generic sitcoms. Fox also offered up *21 Jump Street*, a teen-oriented cop series which turned Johnny Depp into a teen idol. Popular new network series included *A Different World*, a *Cosby Show* spin-off starring Lisa Bonet, and **Thirtysomething**, a drama that followed the interconnected lives of seven adult friends.

'87 *Barfly* Mickey Rourke.

'87 Number One at sixteen—Tiffany.

'87 *Dirty Dancing*—Patrick Swayze and Jennifer Grey.

Welcome to the **Land of thirtysomethings.** For the first time in US history, the median age of American citizens was now over thirty-two. **The baby boomers were creating a baby boom of their own, with a record 3.8 million births in 1988,** but parental roles were changing; according to the Census Bureau, over fifty percent of all new mothers were remaining in the work force.

88

With more and more Americans abandoning their farms (or getting them foreclosed on), the country's farm population was now at its lowest in one hundred and twenty-five years. Another sign of changing times was the closing of the last **Playboy Club**, in Lansing, Michigan. Playboy clubs, which had boasted a membership of over one million men during the early seventies, were considered an embarrassing anachronism by the time the eighties rolled around. In an effort to shore up *Playboy*'s declining fortunes (which included a massive circulation drop in the wake of the Meese Commission's war on pornography) the company decided to phase out the clubs entirely.

Morals Outraged

Playboy (along with every other publication in the country) could at least take heart in the US Supreme Court decision of February 24, which ruled that **free speech** has to be protected even when it is "outrageous," and that the right to criticize public figures is part of free

speech. The ruling overturned a two-hundred-thousand-dollar libel award to Moral Majority leader Rev Jerry Falwell, who had sued *Hustler* magazine over an insulting parody of himself.

On November 18, President Reagan signed an anti-drug bill calling for the death penalty for drug-related murders, and a ten-thousand-dollar fine for possession of even small amounts of controlled substances. A cabinet-level "Drug Czar" position was also established to oversee the **"war on drugs**.

'88 With thawing East-West relations, McDonald's open in Moscow, and the "Bolshoi Mak" is born.

Movie News

Falwell and his colleagues had plenty to get upset about in 1988. Not only was leading televangelist Jimmy Swaggart very publicly defrocked for committing "lewd acts" with a prostitute, but Martin Scorsese's *The Last Temptation of Christ* was committing **blasphemy** by bringing

its depiction of a sensual, all-too-human Jesus Christ to movie theaters everywhere. At least, that's what the Christian Right claimed; most of the fundamentalist Protestants and Roman Catholics who picketed the film's screenings hadn't actually seen it. The film, which received mixed reviews from secular critics, further solidified Willem Dafoe's status as one of the decade's top leading men.

With its eye-popping blend of live action and animation, ***Who Framed Roger Rabbit*** was one of the year's biggest hits, making the curvaceous Jessica Rabbit America's first cartoon sex symbol since Betty Boop. *Hairspray*, a hilarious send-up of early-sixties dance shows, was John Waters' finest commercial work to date; sadly, longtime co-conspirator Divine (who had a starring role) died just as the film was being released. Other hits included *Working Girl* (starring Melanie Griffith as a naive secretary), ***Big*** (starring Tom Hanks as a twelve-year-

'88 Willem Dafoe stars in *The Last Temptation of Christ*.

old boy who suddenly turns into a thirty-year-old man), and *Dangerous Liaisons*, an eighteenth-century costumer which showed that bed-hopping wasn't just an invention of the 1960s.

Tom Cruise, having played a hot-shot jet pilot in *Top Gun* and a hot-shot pool player in *The Color of Money*, now essayed the part of a hot-shot bartender in *Cocktail*. Such redundant role choices didn't hurt his massive popularity any, although *Rain Man* (in which he played the selfish younger brother of the autistic Dustin Hoffman) proved that he could at least stretch a bit. Arnold Schwarzenegger, who showed a flair for droll one-liners in his previous action roles, successfully ventured into the world of comedy with **Twins**. Sylvester Stallone hoped that *Rambo III* would reverse his declining box-office fortunes, but the film's plot (Rambo goes to Afghanistan to blow up the Russians) didn't quite resonate with audiences in the same way its

predecessor had. Jean-Claude Van Damme, the latest inarticulate man of steel to grace the screen, scored action hits with *Bloodsport* and *Black Eagle*.

TV News

With 52.8 percent of all American households having cable TV, 56 percent owning VCRs, and over twenty-five thousand video stores nationwide, network ratings took a serious hit in 1988. When the fall TV season was delayed by a writer's strike, many viewers tuned out completely. Two of the year's few bright spots, as far as commercial television was concerned, were *Murphy Brown* and **Roseanne**. The former starred Candice Bergen as a TV news reporter fresh out of rehab; the latter starred comedienne Roseanne Barr as a working-class mother of three. With their charismatic stars and sharper-than-average writing, both new shows quickly established dedicated followings.

Wrestling Revival

In terms of sheer theatricality, Broadway had nothing on professional wrestling. The sport was at its most popular in three

decades, and wrestlers like Hulk Hogan and "Rowdy" Roddy Piper experienced the sort of name recognition that would have turned "Gorgeous George" Wagner green with envy.

Videogames

Tetris was the video puzzle game that eveyone was playing in 1988. Despite Tetris's popularity, Nintendo stayed at the top of the videogame heap, thanks to the popularity of the company's new Adventures of Link (Zelda 2) and Super Mario 2.

Music News

Heavy metal was bringing in more bucks than ever in 1988, but a Los Angeles band called Guns N' Roses

'88 Many Americans identified with *Roseanne*'s Conor family.

was quickly changing the face and sound of the music. Instead of lipstick, teased hair, and spandex, the band favored leathers, bandanas, and a fresh-from-the-gutter mien; instead of using pointy guitars to crank out catchy bubblegum anthems, Guns N' Roses brandished Les Pauls and sang songs about heroin abuse. Along with **Public Enemy**'s *It Takes A Nation Of Millions To Hold Us Back* (a groundbreaking rap album that mixed articulate rage with an overwhelming sonic barrage of tape loops, big beats, and samples), GNR's *Appetite For Destruction* was a welcome relief from the saccharine pap currently cluttering the airwaves. Jazz vocalist Bobby McFerrin had a fluke pop hit with "**Don't Worry, Be Happy**," a song George Bush would later try to appropriate as the theme for his 1992 campaign.

'88 King of the ring Hulk Hogan.

Talk about good timing—just as Ronald Reagan began his first term with the release of the Iranian Embassy hostages, George Bush made it into the White House only a few months before the **collapse of Communism** in Eastern Europe. Whether the Cold War was brought to an end by the Reagan administration's exorbitant weapons spending, or just by an increasing lust behind the Iron Curtain for blue jeans, bad rock 'n' roll (Russian underground rock hero Boris Grebenshikov made his American debut with 1989's "Radio Silence", which sounded suspiciously like Bryan Adams) and other capitalist luxuries, **America was now rid of its foremost foe.**

TOP TELEVISION SHOWS

Roseanne
The Cosby Show
Cheers
A Different World
The Golden Girls

ACADEMY AWARDS

BEST PICTURE
Driving Miss Daisy
directed by Bruce Beresford

BEST ACTOR
Daniel Day-Lewis
My Left Foot

Best Actress
Jessica Tandy
Driving Miss Daisy

O f course, this created a bit of a problem for defense contractors; deprived of the Red Menace, the defense industry found it increasingly difficult to justify its own existence. But many Americans hoped that, with Communism out of the way, the US government would pay a little more attention to problems on the home front. Unemployment was down slightly in 1989, but most of the 2.5 million new jobs created during the year were in the service industry, rather than in manufacturing. The population of **federal prisons** had nearly doubled since 1980, and a recent educational survey showed that thirteen-year-old students in South Korea, Great Britain, Ireland, Spain, and four Canadian provinces all ranked higher in math and science than Americans of the same age group.

Exhibitionism

Unfortunately, Congress seemed far more preoccupied with a debate over whether or not the National Endowment for the Arts should fund so-called "offensive" art. One casualty of this controversy was an exhibition

of photographs by the late Robert Mapplethorpe, which was slated to open in June at Washington DC's Corocoran Gallery of Art, but was canceled when certain politicos objected to the gay S&M themes of some of the photographs. The Washington Project for the Arts, a private group, wound up taking over the exhibit and opening it in their own facilities.

Thinking Big

Given the eighties' reputation as "the greed decade," it was only fitting that 1989 would witness two of the biggest corporate mergers to date. The merger of Warner Communications and Time, Inc. created Time-Warner, Inc., the world's largest media and entertainment conglomerate, and Kohlberg Kravis and Roberts, which had acquired the Beatrice Companies in 1986, acquired RJR Nabisco for twenty-five billion dollars. The combination of Beatrice and Nabisco properties meant that KKR now accounted for thirteen percent of all US food manufacturing. Luxury hotel owner Leona Helmsley made headlines when she was indicted for tax evasion; according to court

January 2 – The US and Canada sign a comprehensive free trade agreement, which eliminates tariffs and other barriers to trade and investment.

January 4 – US warplanes shoot down two Libyan fighters in international waters off the coast of Libya. Libya claims their planes were unarmed and on a routine patrol; the US claims the planes were armed and trailing the American planes in a hostile fashion.

January 20 – George Bush is inaugurated as America's 41st president.

March 24 – The supertanker *Exxon Valdez* runs aground on Prince William Sound in southeastern Alaska, spilling 240,000 barrels of oil into the water. According to reports, the ship's captain had been drinking, leaving an uncertified officer at the helm at the time of the accident. Exxon agrees to provide $1 billion over the next decade to help clean up the spill, which spread over 730 miles of Alaskan coastline and endangered an estimated 400,000 birds and animals.

April 19 – An explosion on board the US battleship *Iowa* kills 47 sailors. The ship was 300 miles north of Puerto Rico at the time. The Navy initially blames the explosion on a suicide attempt by a crewman, but later retracts the statement under legal pressure from the sailor's family.

July 10 – Rev Jerry Falwell officially disbands the Moral Majority, stating that his goal—getting fundamentalist Christians involved in national politics—has been achieved.

transcripts, Leona's response to the charges was, **"Only little people pay taxes."** Little people everywhere rejoiced when she was sentenced to four years in prison, fined $7.2 million, and ordered to perform seventy-five hours of community service.

Batmania

1989 box-office receipts totalled a record five billion dollars; *Batman*, Tim Burton's incredibly over-hyped adaptation of the DC comic, accounted for roughly half of that. Indeed, with one hundred and sixty varieties of merchandise on the shelves (including T-shirts, coffee mugs, action figures, and separate soundtacks by Prince and Danny Elfman), it was impossible to go anywhere without having the stylized Batman logo stare you in the face.

'89 *Opposite*: **Batman confronts The Joker.**

Though it featured atmospheric sets and Jack Nicholson in fine scenery-chewing form as The Joker, the film suffered from a lousy script and a wooden performance by Michael Keaton in the title role. Still, Batman's runaway success ensured that a sequel would be along shortly.

Other **over-hyped and under-written** hits included *Indiana Jones and the Last Crusade* and *Ghostbusters II*, but 1989 still had more than its share of filmic highlights. Steven

'89 Sally (Meg Ryan) meets Harry (Billy Crystal).

'89 **The establishment did wrong by Spike Lee's** *Do the Right Thing.*

Soderbergh's sharply scripted *sex, lies, and videotape* was a surprise hit, and Gus Van Sant's **Drugstore Cowboy** (starring Matt Dillon in one of his finest performances) looked at drug abuse with such an non-judgmental eye that it was hard to believe the film was made during the Reagan-Bush era. Michael Moore explored the closing of a General Motors plant in the darkly humorous semidocumentary *Roger & Me*, **Meg Ryan** faked an orgasm in a delicatessen in *When Harry Met Sally*, and in *The Fabulous Baker Boys*, Michelle Pfeiffer firmly established her place in the Hollywood firmament with an unbelievably sexy rendition of "Makin' Whoopee." Best of all was Spike Lee's angry and poetic **Do the Right Thing**, though it was snubbed by the Academy of Motion Picture Arts and Sciences, which failed to even honor it with a "Best Picture" nomination.

Excellent!

Disney cleaned up with *The Little Mermaid*, a cartoon loosely based on the Hans Christian Andersen story of the same name, and the Rick Moranis vehicle *Honey, I Shrunk the Kids*. Popular teen fare included *Heathers* (starring Winona Ryder and Christian Slater), *Bill and Ted's Excellent Adventure* (with Keanu Reeves), and *Say Anything*, which further increased the popularity of John Cusack.

Lying Lowe

In the year's biggest Hollywood scandal, teen idol Rob Lowe was sued by a woman in Atlanta, Georgia, who claimed that Lowe had coerced her underage daughter into performing sex acts in front of a video camera. Lowe tried to keep a low profile for a while, but bootleg copies of the videotape made the rounds for years afterwards.

Rose Blighted, But Shoe Sales Bloom

In sports, Cincinnati Reds player and manager Pete Rose was banned from baseball for life for betting on baseball games, allegedly including ones by his own team. One of the best players of his (or any other) era, Rose was virtually guaranteed a spot in the Baseball Hall of Fame; unfortunately, the betting scandal all but nullified his chances of getting in. The future looked far more promising for the sports footwear industry; sneaker companies reported sales of more than four hundred million shoes during the year. Converse claimed that children eighteen and under were responsible for fifty-eight percent of their revenues—even though the company's most popular pairs were priced at over a hundred dollars. **Timberland boots** were also selling especially well, thanks to their popularity among hip-hoppers, who regularly wore them with extra-baggy jeans and triple-fat goosedown coats.

Music News

With new releases as disparate as De La Soul's groovy *Three Feet High and Rising* and NWA's incendiary *Straight Outta Compton*, rap music provided 1989 with its most stimulating sounds. Even novelty rap singles like Young MC's "Bust A Move," 2 Live Crew's "Me So Horny," and Tone Loc's "Funky Cold Medina" were preferable to the **bland pop** of Paula Abdul, Richard Marx, and New Kids on the Block, who dominated the charts for most of the year. Madonna went brunette and made *Like A Prayer*, her strongest album to date, while former New Edition vocalist Bobby Brown left his teeny-bopper past behind him with the tough *Don't Be Cruel*. Harry Connick, Jr, a twenty-two-year-old jazz pianist from New Orleans, became the crooner of the hour, thanks to the success of the *When Harry Met Sally* soundtrack. When Guns N' Roses had an all-acoustic hit with "Patience," a lightbulb went on above MTV's progammers, and "**MTV Unplugged**" debuted in November with a performance by singer-songwriter Jules Shear. An ideal way to resuscitate flagging careers, the show would inspire a spate of "Unplugged" albums throughout the nineties.

'89 Bill and Ted (Alex Winter and Keanu Reeves), ready for adventure.

'89 Nintendo's obsessively popular Game Boy started life in 1989.

around for a few years; *Rescue 911*, hosted by William Shatner, was CBS's popular response to shows like *Cops*. But for the most part, syndicated talk show hosts Arsenio Hall (who became the first black man to host a successful late-night talk show) and Oprah Winfrey (dubbed "**the richest woman on television**" by *TV Guide*) were among the few who could honestly say that they'd had a good year.

IN THE NEWS

August 9 – President Bush signs a bill appropriating $166 billion over ten years for the bail-out of troubled savings and loan associations; 75 percent of the money will be taken from the income taxes of US citizens.

September 28 – The FDA announces that it will allow dideoxyinosine (DDI), an experimental AIDS drug, to be prescribed to AIDS patients while it is still being tested. To date, over 106,000 cases of AIDS have been reported, and over 61,000 Americans have died of the disease.

October 17 – A 6.9 earthquake hits San Francisco, killing 66, most of whom die when a double-decker freeway bridge collapses. The damage is estimated at $10 billion, and the World Series between the San Francisco Giants and the Oakland A's has to be postponed for over a week.

November 11–12 – The Berlin Wall is torn down, symbolically marking the end of the Cold War.

December 3 – President Bush and Soviet president Mikhail Gorbachev have their first summit meeting, in the harbor of Valetta, Malta. Both presidents make statements agreeing that the Cold War is finally over.

December 20 – 24,000 American soldiers invade Panama, in an attempt to overthrow military dictator Manuel Noriega. 23 Americans are killed and 323 wounded in the fighting, which ends on January 3, 1990, with Noriega's capture.

TV News

With 56.4 percent of American households subscribing to cable TV, and 62 percent now owning VCRs, ABC, CBS, and NBC all lost viewers for the sixth consecutive year. The young Fox network also chipped away at the Big Three, thanks to popular "reality" shows like *Cops*, *Totally Hidden Video*, and *America's Most Wanted*, and viewers were further distracted by such pay-per-view events as **Thunder and Mud**, a women's mud-wrestling special hosted by former Jim Bakker paramour Jessica Hahn. Teenagers, who could normally be

counted on to watch almost anything, were busy playing with Nintendo's hand-held **Game Boy**, Atari's portable Lynx, or Sega's Genesis system, which included a version of the popular arcade game Altered Beast.

Talk Isn't Cheap

Two of the year's more popular non-sitcom network offerings were NBC's *LA Law* and ABC's nostalgic *The Wonder Years*, both of which had already been

Lucy And Mel Mourned

1989 also witnessed the deaths of two of television's most significant early stars. Lucille Ball passed away on April 25, aged seventy-seven, and Mel Blanc, the voice of Bugs Bunny, Daffy Duck, Porky Pig and the rest of Warner Brothers' cartoon menagerie, died July 10 at age eighty-one. His headstone inscription? "**That's all, folks!**"

TOP SINGLES

PHIL COLLINS
"Another Day In Paradise"

JANET JACKSON
"Miss You Much"

PAULA ABDUL
"Straight Up"

RICHARD MARX
"Right Here Waiting"

MADONNA
"Like A Prayer"

'89 Oprah—undisputed queen of the talk show.

Index

Acknowledgements

The publishers would like to thank the following sources for their kind permission to reproduce the pictures in this book:

The Advertising Archives

Corbis/J M Chenet, Everett/*Mommie Dearest* Paramount/Frank Yablans, *Conan The Barbarian* Dino de Laurentiis/Edward R. Pressman, *Top Gun* Paramount/Don Simpson, Jerry Bruckheimer, *She's Gotta Have it* Forty Acres And A Mule Filmworks, *Blue Velvet* De Laurentiis, *Roseanne* Viacom, *When Harry Met Sally* Palace/Castle Rock/Nelson Entertainment, *Do The Right Thing* UIP/Forty Acres And A Mule Filmworks/Spike Lee

Ronald Grant Archive/*Sophie's Choice* Universal/AFD/ITC/Keith Barish, *Scarface* Howard Hughes, *This Is Spinal Tap* Mainline/Embassy, *Purple Rain* Columbia-EMI-Warner, *Barfly* Cannon/Barbet Schroeder/ Fred Roos, Tom Luddy, *Last Temptation of Christ* Universal/Cineplex Odeon, *Blade Runner* Warner/Ladd/Blade Runner Partnership,

London Features International Ltd./Agencja Piekna, Angie, Neil Leifer/Camera 5, Phil Loftus, K Regan/Camera 5, A Vereecke, T*he Blues Brothers* Universal, *Raiders Of The Lost Ark* MPTV/Paramount/Lucasfilm, e.t. Universal/Steven Spielberg, Kathleen Kennedy, *Beverly Hills Cop* Paramount/Don Simpson/Jerry Bruckheimer, *Bill & Ted's Excellent Adventure* P Caruso, *Batman Returns* Warner ©1999 MTV Networks Europe. All Rights Reserved. MTV: Music TelevisionR MTV: Music Television and all related titles, logos and characters are trademarks owned and licensed for use by MTV Networks, a division of Viacom International Inc.

Courtesy Nintendo

Pictorial Press Ltd./9 to 5 TCF/IPC, *The Terminator* Orion/Hemdale/Pacific Western, *Rambo* Anabasis Investments NV/Buzz Feitshans, *The Breakfast Club* A&M/Universal, *Fatal Attraction* Paramount/Jaffe-Lansing, *Dirty Dancing* Vestron, Courtesy Sony Computer Entertainment

Every effort has been made to acknowledge correctly and contact the source and/or copyright holder of each picture, and Carlton Books Limited apologises for any unintentional errors or omissions which will be corrected in future editions of this book.

About the Author

Dan Epstein is an award-winning freelance writer and editor who has contributed to many magazines. Since graduating in Film Studies from Vassar College in New York, he has worked for *Chicago Subnation*, a bi-monthly magazine devoted to the city's popular culture, and for the *Los Angeles Reader*. He has also had his work published in *Guitar Player*, *LA Weekly*, *Mojo*, and *Time Out Guide* to Los Angeles.